This journal belongs to

Serenity Journal

Compiled by Barbara Farmer
Designed by Lisa & Jeff Franke

ISBN 978-1-934770-24-5

Printed in China

Serenity

JOURNAL

Ellie Claire
gift & paper expressions

...inspired by life

God grant me the serenity to
accept the things I cannot change;
Courage to change the things I can;
and wisdom to know the difference.

Living one day at a time;
enjoying one moment at a time;
accepting hardships as the pathway to peace;
taking, as He did, this sinful world
as it is, not as I would have it;

Trusting that He will make all things right
if I surrender to His Will;
that I may be reasonably happy in this life
and supremely happy with Him
forever in the next.
Amen.

God grant me the serenity to accept the things I cannot change...

There's a quiet, serene confidence in knowing that all things do not stand or fall according to one's own achievements or the correctness of every decision one makes.

JOSEPH A. SITTLER

A man's heart plans his way, but the Lord directs his steps.

PROVERBS 16:9 NKJV

God grant me the serenity to accept the things I cannot change...

As we practice the presence of God, more and more we find ourselves going through the stresses and strains of daily activity with an ease and serenity that amaze even us...especially us.

RICHARD J. FOSTER

A hostile world! I call to God, I cry to God to help me. From His palace He hears my call; my cry brings me right into His presence—a private audience!

PSALM 18:6 THE MESSAGE

God grant me the serenity to accept the things I cannot change...

No matter how long we are on this earth, the more we have to realize that life finds us living every day with the unanswered and the unresolved. Faith helps us to live with the unanswered. Hope helps us to live with the unresolved. Trust helps us to accept...and go on with the work of living.

MARK CONNOLLY

Love patiently accepts all things. It always trusts,
always hopes, and always endures.

1 CORINTHIANS 13:7 NCV

God grant me the serenity to accept the things I cannot change...

The best reason to pray is that God is really there. In praying, our unbelief gradually starts to melt. God moves smack into the middle of even an ordinary day.... Prayer is a matter of keeping at it.... Thunderclaps and lightning flashes are very unlikely. It is well to start small and quietly.

EMILY GRIFFIN

I pray...that the eyes of your heart may be enlightened in order that
you may know the hope to which He has called you.

EPHESIANS 1:18 NIV

God grant me the serenity to accept the things I cannot change...

My y purpose in writing is to encourage you and assure you that what you are experiencing is truly part of God's grace for you. Stand firm in this grace.

1 Peter 5:12 nlt

God grant me the serenity to accept the things I cannot change...

You can't change circumstances and you can't change other people, but God can change you.

EVELYN A. THEISSEN

*T*he Lord is not slow in doing what He promised—the way some people understand slowness. But God is being patient with you. He does not want anyone to be lost, but He wants all people to change their hearts and lives.

2 PETER 3:9 NCV

*God grant me the serenity to accept
the things I cannot change...*

*T*here are two ways of meeting difficulties. You alter the difficulties or
you alter yourself to meet them.

*C*onsider it pure joy, my brothers, whenever you face trials of many kinds, because you know that the testing of your faith develops perseverance.

JAMES 1:2-3 NIV

God grant me the serenity to
accept the things I cannot change;
Courage to change the things I can;
and wisdom to know the difference.

Living one day at a time;
enjoying one moment at a time;
accepting hardships as the pathway to peace;
taking, as He did, this sinful world
as it is, not as I would have it;

Trusting that He will make all things right
if I surrender to His Will;
that I may be reasonably happy in this life
and supremely happy with Him
forever in the next.
Amen.

*God grant me courage
to change the things I can...*

---

*N*othing is more exciting and rewarding than the sudden flash of insight
that leaves you a changed person.

ARTHUR GORDON

You changed my sorrow into dancing. You took away my
clothes of sadness, and clothed me in happiness.

PSALM 30:11 NCV

God grant me courage
to change the things I can...

God often uses our circumstances to change us as well as
using us to change our circumstances.

There is wonderful joy ahead, even though you have to endure many trials for a little while. These trials will show that your faith is genuine.... So when your faith remains strong through many trials, it will bring you much praise.

1 Peter 1:6-7 nlt

*God grant me courage
to change the things I can...*

Change that which can be altered, explain that which can be understood,
teach that which can be learned, resolve that which can be settled,
and negotiate that which is open to compromise.

JAMES DOBSON

Do the things that show you really have changed your hearts and lives.

MATTHEW 3:8 NCV

God grant me courage
to change the things I can...

The God who created, names, and numbers the stars in the heavens also numbers the hairs of my head.... He pays attention to very big things and to very small ones. What matters to me matters to Him, and that changes my life.

ELISABETH ELLIOT

*G*od's gifts and God's call are under full warranty—
never canceled, never rescinded.

ROMANS 11:29 THE MESSAGE

God grant me courage
to change the things I can...

Everybody thinks of changing humanity and nobody thinks of changing himself.

LEO TOLSTOY

A person with a changed heart seeks praise from God, not from people.

ROMANS 2:29 NLT

*God grant me courage
to change the things I can...*

Choices can change our lives profoundly. The choice to mend a broken relationship, to say "yes" to a difficult assignment, to lay aside some important work to play with a child, to visit some forgotten person—these small choices may affect many lives eternally.

GLORIA GAITHER

*W*ise choices will watch over you. Understanding will keep you safe.

PROVERBS 2:11 NLT

*God grant me courage
to change the things I can...*

Only in growth, reform, and change, paradoxically enough,
is true security to be found.

ANNE MORROW LINDBERGH

*W*here the Spirit of the Lord is, there is freedom. And we, who with unveiled faces all reflect the Lord's glory, are being transformed into His likeness with ever-increasing glory, which comes from the Lord, who is the Spirit.

2 CORINTHIANS 3:17-18 NIV

God grant me the serenity to
accept the things I cannot change;
Courage to change the things I can;
and wisdom to know the difference.

Living one day at a time;
enjoying one moment at a time;
accepting hardships as the pathway to peace;
taking, as He did, this sinful world
as it is, not as I would have it;

Trusting that He will make all things right
if I surrender to His Will;
that I may be reasonably happy in this life
and supremely happy with Him
forever in the next.
Amen.

*God grant me wisdom
to know the difference...*

𝒜lthough we cannot change the direction of the wind,
we can adjust our sails.

If we hope for what we do not see, we eagerly wait for it with perseverance.

ROMANS 8:25 NKJV

*God grant me wisdom
to know the difference...*

What steps of wisdom leads us to a place of trust? Let us look for what is good in our situation. Minimize what is bad. Calmly, quietly trust in God. Relax and let God take full control. Yes, quietly trust.

THELMA MCMILLAN

*R*emember your leaders, who spoke the word of God to you.
Consider the outcome of their way of life and imitate their faith.
Jesus Christ is the same yesterday and today and forever.

HEBREWS 13:7-8 NIV

*God grant me wisdom
to know the difference...*

In darkness there is no choice. It is light that enables us to see the differences between things; and it is Christ who gives us light.

AUGUSTUS W. HARE

Every good and perfect gift is from above, coming down from the Father of the heavenly lights, who does not change like shifting shadows.

JAMES 1:17 NIV

*God grant me wisdom
to know the difference...*

When we live life centered around what others like, feel, and say, we lose touch with our own identity. I am an eternal being, created by God. I am an individual with purpose. It's not what I get from life, but who I am, that makes the difference.

NEVA COYLE

*D*o not conform any longer to the pattern of this world, but be transformed by the renewing of your mind. Then you will be able to test and approve what God's will is—His good, pleasing and perfect will.

ROMANS 12:2 NIV

_God grant me wisdom
to know the difference..._

_**K**indness is more important than wisdom, and the recognition of this
is the beginning of wisdom._

THEODORE ISAAC RUBIN

The wisdom from above is first of all pure. It is also peace loving, gentle at all times, and willing to yield to others. It is full of mercy and good deeds. It shows no favoritism and is always sincere.

JAMES 3:17 NLT

*God grant me wisdom
to know the difference...*

How you do something and the attitude with which you do it are
usually even more important than what you do.... Often we have no
choice about doing things, but we can always choose how to do them.
And that...can make all the difference in your daily life.

NORMAN VINCENT PEALE

Is there any encouragement from belonging to Christ? Any comfort from His love? Any fellowship together in the Spirit? Are your hearts tender and compassionate? Then make me truly happy by...loving one another, and working together with one mind and purpose.

PHILIPPIANS 2:1-2 NLT

God grant me wisdom
to know the difference...

---

*S*ometimes it is necessary for us to speak. At other times it is important that we be quiet. Wisdom comes with knowing the difference.

MRS. D. E. CLAY

*T*here is a time for everything, and everything on earth has its special season....
There is a time to be silent and a time to speak.

ECCLESIASTES 3:1, 7 NCV

God grant me the serenity to
accept the things I cannot change;
Courage to change the things I can;
and wisdom to know the difference.

Living one day at a time;
enjoying one moment at a time;
accepting hardships as the pathway to peace;
taking, as He did, this sinful world
as it is, not as I would have it;

Trusting that He will make all things right
if I surrender to His Will;
that I may be reasonably happy in this life
and supremely happy with Him
forever in the next.
Amen.

To live one day at a time....

Live today! Live fully each moment of today. Trust God to let you work through this moment and the next. He will give you all you need. Don't skip over the painful or confusing moment—even it has its important and rightful place in the day.

People who don't know God and the way He works fuss over these things, but you know both God and how He works. Steep yourself in God-reality, God-initiative, God-provisions. You'll find all your everyday human concerns will be met.

LUKE 12:30-31 THE MESSAGE

To live one day at a time....

Don't just get older, get better. Live realistically. Give generously.
Adapt willingly. Trust fearlessly. Rejoice daily.

CHARLES SWINDOLL

I pray that God, the source of hope, will fill you completely with joy and peace because you trust in Him. Then you will overflow with confident hope through the power of the Holy Spirit.

ROMANS 15:13 NLT

To live one day at a time....

The wonder of living is held within the beauty of silence,
the glory of sunlight...the sweetness of fresh spring air,
the quiet strength of earth, and the love that lies
at the very root of all things.

I pray that from His glorious, unlimited resources He will empower you with inner strength through His Spirit. Then Christ will make His home in your hearts as you trust in Him. Your roots will grow down into God's love and keep you strong.

EPHESIANS 3:16-17 NLT

To live one day at a time...

Face the work of every day with the influence of a few thoughtful, quiet moments with your heart and God.

L. B. COWMAN

Tell me in the morning about Your love, because I trust You.
Show me what I should do, because my prayers go up to You.

PSALM 143:8 NCV

To live one day at a time....

_____

_____

_____

_____

_____

_____

_____

_____

_____

_____

The best thing about the future is that
it comes only one day at a time.

ABRAHAM LINCOLN

God is keeping careful watch over us and the future. The Day is coming when you'll have it all—life healed and whole.

1 PETER 1:5 THE MESSAGE

To live one day at a time....

Every day we live is a priceless gift of God, loaded with possibilities to learn something new, to gain fresh insights.

DALE EVANS ROGERS

Joyful is the person who finds wisdom, the one who gains understanding. For wisdom is more profitable than silver, and her wages are better than gold.

PROVERBS 3:13-14 NLT

To live one day at a time....

*L*ord...give me the gift of faith to be renewed and shared with others each day. Teach me to live this moment only, looking neither to the past with regret, nor the future with apprehension. Let love be my aim and my life a prayer.

ROSEANN ALEXANDER-ISHAM

"*You* shall love the Lord your God with all your heart, with all your soul, and with all your mind." This is the first and great commandment. And the second is like it: "You shall love your neighbor as yourself."

MATTHEW 22:37-39 NKJV

God grant me the serenity to
accept the things I cannot change;
Courage to change the things I can;
and wisdom to know the difference.

Living one day at a time;
enjoying one moment at a time;
accepting hardships as the pathway to peace;
taking, as He did, this sinful world
as it is, not as I would have it;

Trusting that He will make all things right
if I surrender to His Will;
that I may be reasonably happy in this life
and supremely happy with Him
forever in the next.
Amen.

To enjoy one moment at a time...

Don't ever let yourself get so busy that you miss those little but important extras in life–the beauty of a day...the smile of a friend...the serenity of a quiet moment alone. For it is often life's smallest pleasures and gentlest joys that make the biggest and most lasting difference.

The Lord is my shepherd, I shall not be in want. He makes me lie down in green pastures, He leads me beside quiet waters, He restores my soul.

PSALM 23:1-3 NIV

To enjoy one moment at a time...

Be still, and in the quiet moments, listen to the voice of your heavenly Father. His words can renew your spirit...no one knows you and your needs like He does.

JANET WEAVER SMITH

I'm asking God for one thing, only one thing: To live with Him in His house my whole life long. I'll contemplate His beauty; I'll study at His feet. That's the only quiet, secure place in a noisy world.

PSALM 27:4-5 THE MESSAGE

To enjoy one moment at a time...

Our days are filled with tiny golden minutes with eternity in them....
One thousand years from this day you will be more alive than you are at this
moment. There is a future life with God for those who put their trust in Him.

BILLY GRAHAM

*L*et all that I am wait quietly before God, for my hope is in Him.
He alone is my rock and my salvation.

PSALM 62:5-6 NLT

To enjoy one moment at a time...

Let your faith in Christ, the omnipresent One, be in the quiet confidence that He will every day and every moment keep you as the apple of His eye, keep you in perfect peace.

ANDREW MURRAY

*K*eep me as the apple of Your eye; hide me under the shadow of Your wings.

PSALM 17:8 NKJV

To enjoy one moment at a time...

$\mathcal{G}$od is every moment totally aware of each one of us. Totally aware in intense concentration and love.... No man passes through any area of life, happy or tragic, without the attention of God with Him.

EUGENIA PRICE

If God gives such attention to the appearance of wildflowers...don't you think He'll attend to you...? What I'm trying to do here is to get you to relax, to not be so preoccupied with *getting*, so you can respond to God's *giving*.

MATTHEW 6:30-31 THE MESSAGE

To enjoy one moment at a time...

Great works do not always lie our way, but every moment we may
do little ones excellently, that is, with great love.

FRANCIS DE SALES

The master answered, "You did well. You are a good and loyal servant.
Because you were loyal with small things, I will let you care for much
greater things. Come and share my joy with me."

MATTHEW 25:23 NCV

To enjoy one moment at a time...

Happy people...enjoy the fundamental, often very simple things of life....
They savor the moment, glad to be alive.... They are adaptable....
Their eyes are turned outward; they are aware, compassionate.
They have the capacity to love.

JANE CANFIELD

But what happens when we live God's way? He brings gifts into our lives, much the same way that fruit appears in an orchard—things like affection for others, exuberance about life, serenity. We develop...a sense of compassion in the heart.

GALATIANS 5:22 THE MESSAGE

God grant me the serenity to
accept the things I cannot change;
Courage to change the things I can;
and wisdom to know the difference.

Living one day at a time;
enjoying one moment at a time;
accepting hardships as the pathway to peace;
taking, as He did, this sinful world
as it is, not as I would have it;

Trusting that He will make all things right
if I surrender to His Will;
that I may be reasonably happy in this life
and supremely happy with Him
forever in the next.
Amen.

To accept hardships as the pathway to peace...

God came to us because God wanted to join us on the road, to listen to our story, and to help us realize that we are not walking in circles but moving toward the house of peace and joy.

HENRI J. M. NOUWEN

Your life is a journey you must travel with a deep consciousness of God.

1 PETER 1:18 THE MESSAGE

To accept hardships as the pathway to peace...

The highest happiness of man is to have probed what is knowable and quietly to revere what is unknowable.

Do you think you can explain the mystery of God? Do you think you can diagram God Almighty? God is far higher than you can imagine, far deeper than you can comprehend.

JOB 11:7-9 THE MESSAGE

To accept hardships as the pathway to peace...

[Trials] may come in abundance. But they cannot penetrate into the sanctuary of the soul when it is settled in God, and we may dwell in perfect peace.

HANNAH WHITALL SMITH

I have told you these things, so that in Me you may have peace. In this world you will have trouble. But take heart! I have overcome the world.

JOHN 16:33 NIV

To accept hardships as the pathway to peace...

Character cannot be developed in ease and quiet. Only through experience of trial and suffering can the soul be strengthened, vision cleared, ambition inspired, and success achieved.

HELEN KELLER

We also rejoice in our sufferings, because we know that suffering produces perseverance; perseverance, character; and character, hope. And hope does not disappoint us.

ROMANS 5:3-5 NIV

To accept hardships as the pathway to peace...

When peace like a river attendeth my way, when sorrow like sea-billows roll;
Whatever my lot, Thou hast taught me to say, "It is well,
it is well with my soul."

HORATIO G. SPAFFORD

*B*e of good comfort, be of one mind, live in peace;
and the God of love and peace will be with you.

2 CORINTHIANS 13:11 NKJV

To accept hardships as the pathway to peace...

There are those who suffer greatly, and yet, through the recognition that pain can be a thread in the pattern of God's weaving, find the way to a fundamental joy.

*O*ut of the most severe trial, their overflowing joy and their
extreme poverty welled up in rich generosity.

2 CORINTHIANS 8:2 NIV

To accept hardships as the pathway to peace...

Peace is not placidity: peace is...The power to endure the megatron of pain
With joy, the silent thunder of release, the ordering of Love.
Peace is the atom's start, The primal image: God within the heart.

MADELEINE L'ENGLE

*M*ay God give you more and more mercy, peace, and love.

JUDE 1:2 NLT

God grant me the serenity to
accept the things I cannot change;
Courage to change the things I can;
and wisdom to know the difference.

Living one day at a time;
enjoying one moment at a time;
accepting hardships as the pathway to peace;
taking, as He did, this sinful world
as it is, not as I would have it;

Trusting that He will make all things right
if I surrender to His Will;
that I may be reasonably happy in this life
and supremely happy with Him
forever in the next.
Amen.

God's peace that passes all understanding...

All [God's] glory and beauty come from within, and there He delights to dwell. His visits there are frequent, His conversation sweet, His comforts refreshing, His peace passing all understanding.

THOMAS À KEMPIS

*I*nstead of worrying, pray. Let petitions and praises shape your worries into prayers, letting God know your concerns. Before you know it, a sense of God's wholeness, everything coming together for good, will come and settle you down.

PHILIPPIANS 4:6-7 THE MESSAGE

God's peace that passes all understanding...

Life from the Center is a life of unhurried peace and power. It is simple.
It is serene.... We need not get frantic. He is at the helm. And when our little
day is done, we lie down quietly in peace, for all is well.

THOMAS R. KELLY

I will both lie down in peace, and sleep; for You alone,
O Lord, make me dwell in safety.

PSALM 4:8 NKJV

God's peace that passes all understanding...

Only God gives true peace—a quiet gift He sets within us just when we think we've exhausted our search for it.

I am leaving you with a gift—peace of mind and heart. And the peace I give
is a gift the world cannot give. So don't be troubled or afraid.

JOHN 14:27 NLT

God's peace that passes all understanding...

*L*ook back from where we have come.... How could we know the joy without the suffering? And how could we endure the suffering but that we are warmed and carried on the breast of God?

DESMOND M. TUTU

*G*od is the Father who is full of mercy and all comfort. He comforts us every time we have trouble.... We share in the many sufferings of Christ. In the same way, much comfort comes to us through Christ.

2 Corinthians 1:3-5 ncv

God's peace that passes all understanding...

Not a sigh is breathed, not a pain felt, not a grief pierces the soul, but the throb vibrates to the Father's heart.

ELLEN G. WHITE

You keep track of all my sorrows. You have collected all my tears in Your bottle. You have recorded each one in Your book.... This I know: God is on my side!

PSALM 56:8-9 NLT

God's peace that passes all understanding...

Let my soul take refuge...beneath the shadow of Your wings:
let my heart, this sea of restless waves, find peace in You, O God.

AUGUSTINE

For You have been my refuge, a strong tower against the foe. I long to dwell in
Your tent forever and take refuge in the shelter of Your wings.

PSALM 61:3-4 NIV

God's peace that passes all understanding...

I abide in Christ and in doing so I find rest, and the peace of God which passes all understanding fills my heart and life.

JOHN HUNTER

Fix your thoughts on what is true, and honorable, and right, and pure, and lovely, and admirable. Think about things that are excellent and worthy of praise.... Then the God of peace will be with you.

PHILIPPIANS 4:8-9 NLT

God grant me the serenity to
accept the things I cannot change;
Courage to change the things I can;
and wisdom to know the difference.

Living one day at a time;
enjoying one moment at a time;
accepting hardships as the pathway to peace;
taking, as He did, this sinful world
as it is, not as I would have it;

Trusting that He will make all things right
if I surrender to His Will;
that I may be reasonably happy in this life
and supremely happy with Him
forever in the next.
Amen.

To take, as Christ did,
this sinful world as it is...

*T*he important thing is not how much we accomplish, but how much love
we put into our deeds every day. That is the measure of our love for God.

MOTHER TERESA

My little children, let us not love in word or in tongue, but in deed
and in truth. And by this we know that we are of the truth,
and shall assure our hearts before Him.

1 JOHN 3:18-19 NKJV

To take, as Christ did,
this sinful world as it is...

*I*t is only when Christ dwells within our hearts, radiating the pure light of His love through our humanity that we discover who we are and what we were intended to be. There is no other joy...that is more complete.

I pray that Christ will live in your hearts by faith and that your life
will be strong in love and be built on love.

EPHESIANS 3:17 NCV

To take, as Christ did,
this sinful world as it is...

The reason we can dare to risk loving others is that "God has for Christ's sake loved us." Think of it! We are loved eternally, totally, individually, unreservedly! Nothing can take God's love away.

GLORIA GAITHER

God demonstrates His own love toward us, in that while
we were still sinners, Christ died for us.

ROMANS 5:8 NKJV

To take, as Christ did,
this sinful world as it is...

God never abandons anyone on whom He has set His love; nor does Christ, the good shepherd, ever lose track of His sheep.

J. I. PACKER

I am the good shepherd. The good shepherd gives His life for the sheep.

JOHN 10:11 NCV

To take, as Christ did,
this sinful world as it is...

God looks at the world through the eyes of love. If we, therefore, as human beings made in the image of God also want to see reality rationally, that is, as it truly is, then we, too, must learn to look at what we see with love.

ROBERTA BONDI

Even before He made the world, God loved us and chose us in Christ
to be holy and without fault in His eyes.

EPHESIANS 1:4 NLT

To take, as Christ did,
this sinful world as it is...

When one has once fully entered the realm of love, the world—
no matter how imperfect—becomes rich and beautiful,
for it consists solely of opportunities for love.

SØREN KIERKEGAARD

*L*et us hold unswervingly to the hope we profess, for He
who promised is faithful. And let us consider how we may
spur one another on toward love and good deeds.

HEBREWS 10:23-24 NIV

To take, as Christ did,
this sinful world as it is...

If Christ lives in us, controlling our personalities, we will leave glorious marks on the lives we touch. Not because of our lovely characters, but because of His.

EUGENIA PRICE

*T*his is my prayer for you: that your love will grow more and more;...
that you will be filled with the good things produced in your life by Christ
to bring glory and praise to God.

PHILIPPIANS 1:9, 11 NCV

God grant me the serenity to
accept the things I cannot change;
Courage to change the things I can;
and wisdom to know the difference.

Living one day at a time;
enjoying one moment at a time;
accepting hardships as the pathway to peace;
taking, as He did, this sinful world
as it is, not as I would have it;

Trusting that He will make all things right
if I surrender to His Will;
that I may be reasonably happy in this life
and supremely happy with Him
forever in the next.
Amen.

To trust that Christ will make all things right...

All the things in this world are gifts and signs of God's love to us.
The whole world is a love letter from God.

PETER KREEFT

God's word is true, and everything He does is right. He loves what is right and fair; the Lord's love fills the earth.

PSALM 33:4-5 NCV

To trust that Christ will make all things right...

God makes a promise—faith believes it, hope anticipates it, patience quietly awaits it.

But we have the true hope that comes from being made right with God, and by the Spirit we wait eagerly for this hope.

GALATIANS 5:5 NCV

To trust that Christ will make all things right...

*God's holy beauty comes near you...and it stirs your drowsing soul....
He creates in you the desire to find Him and run after Him—to follow
wherever He leads you, and to press peacefully against His heart
wherever He is.*

JOHN OF THE CROSS

$\mathscr{S}$eek the Lord your God, and you will find Him if you seek Him with all your heart and with all your soul.

DEUTERONOMY 4:29 NKJV

To trust that Christ will
make all things right...

---

*G*od Incarnate is the end of fear; and the heart that realizes that He
is in the midst, that takes heed to the assurance of His loving presence,
will be quiet in the midst of alarm.

F. B. MEYER

*T*he fruit of righteousness will be peace; the effect of righteousness
will be quietness and confidence forever.

Isaiah 32:17 niv

To trust that Christ will make all things right...

You can trust God right now to supply all your needs for today.
And if your needs are more tomorrow, His supply will be greater also.

And my God shall supply all your need according to
His riches in glory by Christ Jesus.

PHILIPPIANS 4:19 NKJV

To trust that Christ will make all things right...

We don't have to be perfect to be a blessing. We are asked only to be real, trusting in His perfection to cover our imperfection, knowing that one day we will finally be all that Christ saved us for and wants us to be.

GIGI GRAHAM TCHIVIDJIAN

*You will keep in perfect peace him whose mind is steadfast,
because he trusts in You.*

Isaiah 26:3 NIV

To trust that Christ will make all things right...

Lord, grant me a quiet mind, that trusting Thee, for Thou art kind,
I may go on without a fear, for Thou, my Lord, art always near.

AMY CARMICHAEL

The Lord is my light and my salvation; whom shall I fear?
The Lord is the strength of my life; of whom shall I be afraid?

PSALM 27:1 NKJV

God grant me the serenity to
accept the things I cannot change;
Courage to change the things I can;
and wisdom to know the difference.

Living one day at a time;
enjoying one moment at a time;
accepting hardships as the pathway to peace;
taking, as He did, this sinful world
as it is, not as I would have it;

Trusting that He will make all things right
if I surrender to His Will;
that I may be reasonably happy in this life
and supremely happy with Him
forever in the next.
Amen.

Surrendering to His will...

The peacefulness of God's creation reminds us of the spiritual
peace we have when we live in obedience to Him.

JANETTE OKE

*N*ow may God Himself, the God of peace, make you pure, belonging only to Him. May your whole self—spirit, soul, and body—be kept safe and without fault when our Lord Jesus Christ comes. You can trust the One who calls you to do that for you.

1 THESSALONIANS 5:23-24 NCV

Surrendering to His will...

God did not tell us to follow Him because He needed our help,
but because He knew that loving Him would make us whole.

IRENAEUS

This is how much God loved the world: He gave His Son, His one and only Son. And this is why: so that no one need be destroyed; by believing in Him, anyone can have a whole and lasting life.

JOHN 3:16 THE MESSAGE

Surrendering to His will...

The serene beauty of a holy life is the most powerful influence
in the world next to the power of God.

BLAISE PASCAL

*B*lessed are the people who know the passwords of praise, who shout on parade in the bright presence of God…. Your vibrant beauty has gotten inside us—You've been so good to us!… All we are and have we owe to God.

PSALM 89:15, 17-18 THE MESSAGE

Surrendering to His will...

The greatness of a man's power is the measure of his surrender.

WILLIAM BOOTH

We now have this light shining in our hearts, but we ourselves are like fragile clay jars containing this great treasure. This makes it clear that our great power is from God, not from ourselves.

2 CORINTHIANS 4:7 NLT

Surrendering to His will...

Savior, teach me day by day Love's sweet lesson to obey;
Sweeter lesson cannot be, loving Him who first loved me.

JANE E. LEESON

*S*ince you have purified your souls in obeying the truth through the Spirit in sincere love of the brethren, love one another fervently with a pure heart, having been born again...through the word of God which lives and abides forever.

1 PETER 1:22-23 NKJV

Surrendering to His will...

When we walk with the Lord in the light of His Word,
what a glory He sheds on our way!
While we do His good will, He abides with us still,
and with all who will trust and obey.

JOHN STAMMIS

He who dwells in the secret place of the Most High shall abide under the shadow of the Almighty. I will say of the Lord, "He is my refuge and my fortress; my God, in Him I will trust."

PSALM 91:1-2 NKJV

Surrendering to His will...

One thing Jesus asks of me: that I lean upon Him; that in Him alone
I put complete trust; that I surrender myself to Him unreservedly.

MOTHER TERESA

Lord, we show our trust in You by obeying Your laws;
our heart's desire is to glorify Your name.

ISAIAH 26:8 NLT

God grant me the serenity to
accept the things I cannot change;
Courage to change the things I can;
and wisdom to know the difference.

Living one day at a time;
enjoying one moment at a time;
accepting hardships as the pathway to peace;
taking, as He did, this sinful world
as it is, not as I would have it;

Trusting that He will make all things right
if I surrender to His Will;
that I may be reasonably happy in this life
and supremely happy with Him
forever in the next.
Amen.

That I may be reasonably happy in this life...

As we grow in our capacities to see and enjoy the joys that God has placed in our lives, life becomes a glorious experience of discovering His endless wonders.

*Y*ou will show me the path of life; in Your presence is fullness of joy;
at Your right hand are pleasures forevermore.

PSALM 16:11 NKJV

*That I may be reasonably
happy in this life...*

God wants His children to establish such a close relationship with Him that He becomes a natural partner in all the experiences of life. That includes those precious, happy times.

GLORIA GAITHER

May you be filled with joy, always thanking the Father. He has enabled you to share in the inheritance that belongs to His people, who live in the light.

COLOSSIANS 1:11-12 NLT

That I may be reasonably happy in this life...

I asked God for all things that I might enjoy life. He gave me life that I might enjoy all things.

The God who made the whole world and everything in it is the Lord of the land and the sky. He does not live in temples built by human hands. This God is the One who gives life, breath, and everything else to people.

ACTS 17:24-25 NCV

That I may be reasonably
happy in this life...

Our hearts were made for joy and to enjoy the One who created them.
Too deeply planted to be much affected by the ups and downs of life,
this joy is a knowing and a being known by our Creator.
He sets our hearts alight with radiant joy.

The revelation of God is whole and pulls our lives together.
The signposts of God are clear and point out the right road.
The life-maps of God are right, showing the way to joy.

PSALM 19:7-8 THE MESSAGE

That I may be reasonably happy in this life...

If God is not lost in our lives, if goodness is not lost in our lives,
if memories are not lost in our lives, then we will have an easier time
of finding our way to personal happiness.

CHRISTOPHER DE VINCK

*K*eep on asking, and you will receive what you ask for. Keep on seeking,
and you will find. Keep on knocking, and the door will be opened to you.

MATTHEW 7:7 NLT

That I may be reasonably happy in this life...

*L*ife in the presence of God should be known to us in conscious experience.
It is a life to be enjoyed every moment of every day.

A. W. TOZER

Thank God! Pray to Him by name! Tell everyone you meet what He has done!... Live a happy life! Keep your eyes open for God, watch for His works; be alert for signs of His presence. Remember the world of wonders He has made.

PSALM 105:1, 3-5 THE MESSAGE

That I may be reasonably happy in this life...

If we learn how to give of ourselves, to forgive others, and to live with thanksgiving, we need not seek happiness. It will seek us.

If you cling to your life, you will lose it; but if you give up your life for Me, you will find it.

MATTHEW 10:39 NLT

God grant me the serenity to
accept the things I cannot change;
Courage to change the things I can;
and wisdom to know the difference.

Living one day at a time;
enjoying one moment at a time;
accepting hardships as the pathway to peace;
taking, as He did, this sinful world
as it is, not as I would have it;

Trusting that He will make all things right
if I surrender to His Will;
that I may be reasonably happy in this life
and supremely happy with Him
forever in the next.

Amen.

*To be supremely happy with
my Heavenly Father forever in the next.*

....

....

....

....

....

....

....

....

....

....

....

....

Heaven often seems distant and unknown, but if He who made the road…
is our guide, we need not fear to lose the way.

HENRY VAN DYKE

*J*esus said to him, "I am the way, the truth, and the life. No one comes to the Father except through Me."

JOHN 14:6 NKJV

*To be supremely happy with
my Heavenly Father forever in the next.*

What God does in time, He planned from eternity. And all that He planned
in eternity He carries out in time.... No part of His eternal plan changes.

J. I. PACKER

So keep a firm grip on the faith.... It won't be long before this generous God who has great plans for us in Christ—eternal and glorious plans they are!—will have you put together and on your feet for good. He gets the last word.

1 PETER 5:10-11 THE MESSAGE

*To be supremely happy with
my Heavenly Father forever in the next.*

Heaven will be the perfection we have always longed for. It will be filled with health, vigor, virility, knowledge, happiness, worship, love, and perfection.

BILLY GRAHAM

We know that our body—the tent we live in here on earth—will be destroyed. But when that happens, God will have a house for us. It will...be a home in heaven that will last forever.

2 CORINTHIANS 5:1 NCV

To be supremely happy with my Heavenly Father forever in the next.

Think of stepping on shore, and finding it Heaven!
Of taking hold of a hand, and finding it God's hand,...
Of passing from storm and tempest to an unbroken calm,
Of waking up, and finding it Home!

In My Father's house are many mansions; if it were not so,
I would have told you. I go to prepare a place for you.
And if I go and prepare a place for you, I will come again and
receive you to Myself; that where I am, there you may be also.

JOHN 14:2-3 NKJV

To be supremely happy with my Heavenly Father forever in the next.

In heaven our light will be provided by an infallible source, the Son of God. And nothing will interfere with our basking in His fellowship.

MARILYN M. MORGAN

The City shimmered like a precious gem, light-filled, pulsing light....
The City doesn't need sun or moon for light. God's Glory
is its light, the Lamb its lamp!

REVELATION 21:12, 23 THE MESSAGE

As we follow Him who is everlasting
we will touch the things that last forever.